HORSEPOWER

FUNNY CARS

by Angie Peterson Kaelberer

Reading Consultant:

Barbara J. Fox

Reading Specialist

North Carolina State University

Capstone press

Mankato, Minnesota

Blazers is published by Capstone Press,
151 Good Counsel Drive, P.O. Box 669, Mankato, Minnesota 56002.
www.capstonepress.com

Library of Congress Cataloging-in-Publication Data
Kaelberer, Angie Peterson.
    Funny cars / by Angie Peterson Kaelberer.
    p. cm.—(Blazers. Horsepower)
    Summary: "Discusses funny cars, including their main features
and how they are raced"—Provided by publisher.
    Includes bibliographical references and index.
    ISBN 0-7368-4389-2 (hardcover)
    ISBN 0-7368-6170-X (softcover)
    1. Funny cars—Juvenile literature. I. Title. II. Series.
TL236.23.K34 2006
629.228—dc22   2005001428

Credits
Jason Knudson, set designer; Patrick D. Dentinger, book designer;
    Kelly Garvin, photo researcher; Scott Thoms, photo editor

Photo Credits
All photos by Auto Imagery Inc.

The publisher does not endorse products whose logos may appear on objects in
images in this book.

**Capstone Press thanks Betty Carlan, Research Librarian at the
International Motorsports Hall of Fame in Talladega, Alabama, for
her assistance in preparing this book.**

1 2 3 4 5 6 10 09 08 07 06 05

TABLE OF CONTENTS

SMOKE AND SPEED

Two funny cars sit at the starting line. The drivers wait for the signal to start the drag race.

The cars speed away in a cloud of smoke. One car crosses the finish line first. The driver wins by less than one second.

BLAZER FACT

Funny cars have parachutes
packed in the rear of the car.
The parachutes slow down
the car at the end of the race.

Parachute

The driver wins all of his races that day. At the end of the day, he has a trophy and a suitcase full of cash.

9

FUNNY CAR DESIGN

Funny cars are dragsters.
They race two at a time on
straight paved tracks.

Funny cars have no trunk, hood, or doors. The outer shell of the car lifts up to let the driver in and out.

Outer shell

Exhaust pipes

Rear deck spoiler

The rear tires are large. A rear
deck spoiler is on the back of the
car. The spoiler helps the rear tires
grip the track.

BLAZER FACT

Funny cars look different from other race cars. Some drivers thought the cars looked funny. The name stuck.

FUNNY CAR DIAGRAM

Rear deck spoiler

Parachutes

Wheelie bar

Window opening

HEMI ENGINES

Huge hemi engines power funny cars. These engines push the cars to high speeds.

Most funny car engines burn nitromethane. This fuel explodes easily. Flames shoot out of the exhaust pipes.

Exhaust pipes

Short races and high speeds damage engines. Crews rebuild engines after each event.

BLAZER FACT

In 2004, John Force set the funny car speed record of 333.58 miles (536.83 kilometers) per hour.

FUNNY CARS IN ACTION

Each round of races is called a heat. The winners move on to the next heat.

Drivers keep racing until only one is left. This driver is the winner.

BLAZER FACT

Funny car drivers need a fast start. Drivers say, "If you see green, you've lost the race."

Starting light

BUILT FOR SPEED!

INDEX